Pretty Origami Flowers

How to Make An Origami Flower

DEDICATION

Contents

Origami Lotus

1. Start with white side up. Fold diagonally both ways and open.

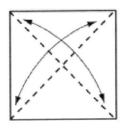

2. Fold each corner into the centre.

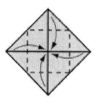

3. Fold each corner into the centre once again.

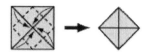

4. For a third time, fold each corner into the centre.

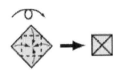

5. Turn model over and fold each corner into the centre.

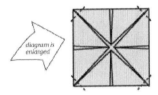

6. Fold each corner inwards a small amount.

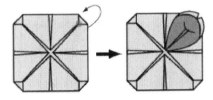

7. To form the petals, press down on the point shown, while slowly pulling the petal from behind, to the front. It's almost like turning the corner "inside out". Repeat on all corners.

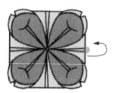

8. The second set of petals are formed the same way, but the corner from the point shown.

9. The third set doesn't need to be turned "inside out", just folded normally from below the first set.

Finished Lotus.

Origami Kusudama Flowers

Supplies:

Origami Paper

Glue - either Elmer's School Glue or a Glue Stick

A Paintbrush (if you're using runny glue)

Regular Printer Paper,

Magazines,

Maps,

Colouring Book Pages,

Old Books,

And Newspapers.

How To Make Origami Kusudama Flowers:

1. To start you'll need to choose your paper. You'll need five square pieces for each flower. Every single sheet of paper makes one petal.

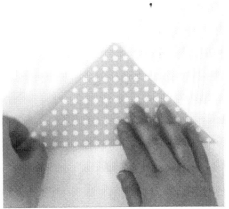

You can experiment with different size papers to see what size flower you like.

2. Take your sheet of square paper and fold it in half along the diagonal

to make a triangle shape. You want the coloured side facing out.

3. Fold both the bottom corners up to meet in the middle and make a diamond shape.

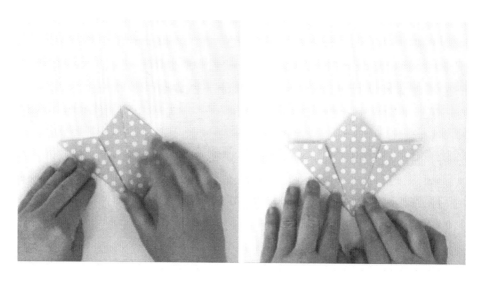

4. Fold both the points back so they line up with outside edge. This will make two pockets.

5. Pop open the pocket using a finger.

6. Flatten along the seam to make a kite shape and squash down.

7. Do the same on the other side.

8. Fold the top of each kite down to make two triangles. You want the top of the triangles to line up with the edge.

9. Take both sides and fold them in half towards the centre.

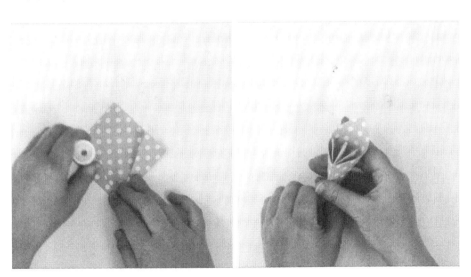

10. Apply glue to one of the flaps.

11. Bring the two sides together so that both the flaps meet.

12. Press together. You may need to hold in place for a minute while the glue sets.

13. You've now made one petal. You can use your fingers to gently neaten up the inner pieces.

14. Repeat the steps above until you have five petals.

15. Take a petal and glue along the join.

16. Join together to a second petal. Hold until the glue sets.

17. Keep adding petals until you've joined five together. You may find it easier to make a 2-petal piece and a 3-petal piece separately and then

glue the 2 pieces together.

18. Set aside to dry.

Origami Lily

Supplies You'll Need

Materials

Colored craft paper

Craft glue

Tools

Scissors

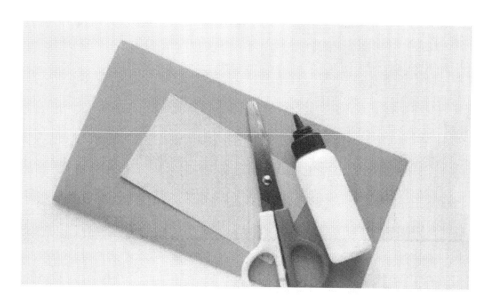

Instructions

Step 1: Base Folds

Prepare a piece of square craft paper. Fold the square paper into half from both sides (vertically and horizontally). Flip the paper to the other side. This time, fold the paper diagonally, from both sides. Draw the diagonal folds upwards and push the vertical-horizontal creases inwards; this will form a star pattern with 4 points/corners.

Step 2: Flatten Base Paper and Form a Triangle Pattern

Now, bring 2 corners /points together and thus divide the 4 corners into 2 groups. Flatten the current pattern. This should form a triangle shape, with 2 flaps on each side.

Step 3: Working on the Triangle Flaps

Take any one of the triangle flaps and hold it at a 90 degrees angle with the rest of the pattern. Hold the closed end of the flap and flatten the flap by keeping its closed-end (outer side) aligned along the middle.

17

Step 4: Flip and Fold Top Corners

The crease of the flattened flap should be aligned right along the middle. Now, rotate the current pattern, drawing the top corner of the main triangle pattern facing down. Now, the current pattern should have 3 corners along the top side. We are going to work with the middle part. Fold the right and left corners (not the top corner) inside and align them with the middle crease.

Step 5: Bring the Top Downwards and Flatten

Now, hold the top corner and draw it all the way to the opposite corner. This part is tricky, carefully and slowly flatten the middle part with the main triangle base.

Step 5 of Making Bring the Top Downwards and Flatten

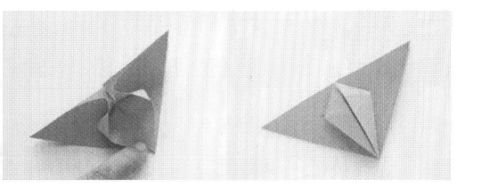

Step 6: Prepare the 3 other Triangle Flaps

One by one fold the rest of the flap following the same technique. This should form a somewhat diamond-shaped pattern. Draw the longer side of the diamond pattern up. The longer side has flaps.

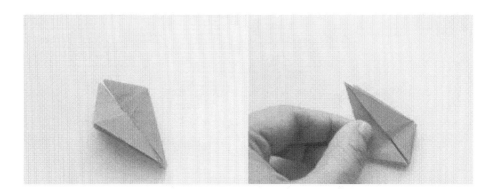

Step 7: Open Vertical Pattern and Fold the Sides Inwards

Draw any one of the flaps all the way to the opposite side. We are going to work with the closed end of the current pattern now. Fold the right and left (top side) corners of the top layer inwards and align them with the middle crease.

Step 8: Prepare the Rest of the Parts Similarly

Similarly, fold the rest of the sides (the pattern has a total of 4 layers/flaps/parts). Now, hold the closed end of the current pattern and keep the open end facing upwards.

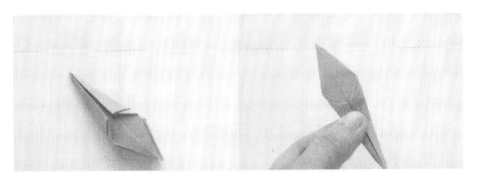

Step 9: Forming the Petals

Carefully open the top layers, these are the petals of our origami flower pattern. There should be a total of 4 petals.

Step 10: Prepare Rest of the Patterns and Assemble

Similarly, craft another piece of origami flower. Take a small piece of yellow paper and ut thin fringes along any one side of the paper. Roll the intact side of the yellow paper and thus, the stamen of the origami lily is ready. Assemble the 2 origami flower patterns together by inserting one inside the other. Insert the papercraft stamen inside the center hole of the top origami flower pattern. If necessary, apply a drop of glue to secure the patterns.

Origami Rose In Bloom

Materials

Colored craft paper

No tools required

Instructions

Step 1: Base Creases

Take the square paper and fold the paper into half from both sides to create criss-cross creases. Flip the paper to the other side and fold the paper in half diagonally from both sides again to create diagonal criss-cross creases on the square paper.

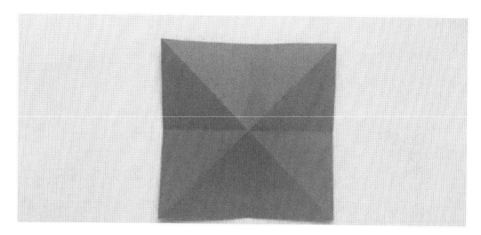

Step 2: The Star Fold

Fold up the diagonal creases and fold the vertical-horizontal creases inwards, this will form a 4 point star pattern.

Step 3: Flattening the Star

Join the adjacent parts of the 4 point star pattern and then flatten the pattern.

Step 4: Fold-Up Bottom Corners

Fold up the bottom corners and join them with the top corner of the current pattern (triangle).

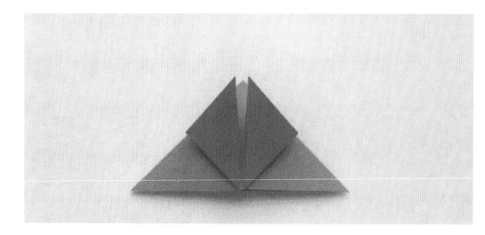

Step 5: Open Corner Pocket

The parts we folded up in the previous step should have pockets on the inner sides. Carefully open the pocket of any one of the sides.

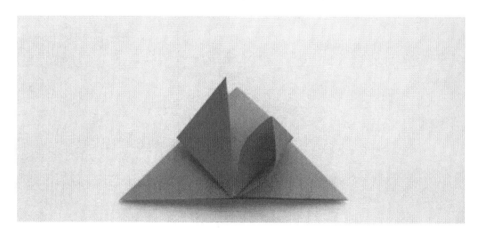

Step 6: Flatten the Corner

Open the pocket as much as you can and then join the corner (the top corner) with the bottom-middle part of teh current pattern. Flatten the pocket with the pattern and it'll form a square part.

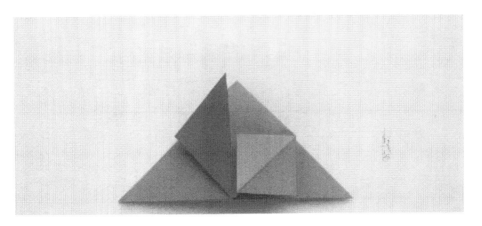

Step 7: Flatten the Other Side

Similarly, open the pocket and flatten it with the current pattern.

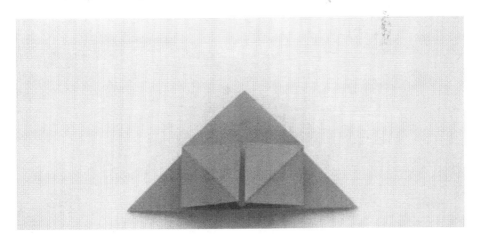

Step 8: Fold-Up 3 Inner Corners

Fold up and join the 2 inner-bottom corners to the opposite (diagonally) corners of each square parts. Half-fold and join the bottom corner of the middle part to its opposite corner.

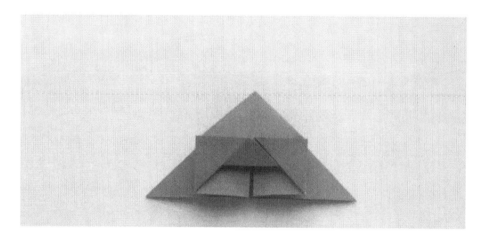

Step 9: Fold the Opposite Side

Turn the current pattern to the other side and similarly fold the other side.

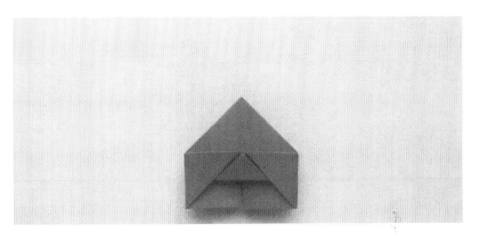

Step 10: Turn the Flaps

The current pattern should have 2 flaps on each side (left and right). Now simply flip and join the flaps with their opposite flap. To be more precise, join the top left flap with the top right flap and then join the bottom left flap with the bottom right flap.

Step 11: Fold-In the Outer Corners

Fold the bottom side corners up.

Step 12: Fold-Up the Bottom Half

Fold up the bottom corner of the middle part.

Step 13: Fold the Other Side

Now, turn the current pattern to the other side and similarly, make the

3 corner folds.

Step 14: The Bottom Side

Hold the current pattern in your hand and bring the bottom side to the front. carefully open the bottom side.

Step 15: Flatten the Bottom Side

Continue to open the bottom pattern until it is completely flat.

Step 16: Hold the Cross-Cross Pattern

Now, turn the pattern to the other side. This side should have a pinty criss-cross pattern. Place 1 finger between every 2 layers.

Step 17: Twist the Criss-Cross Pattern

Now carefully twist the pattern clock-wise. While twisting the pattern make sure to hold the flat bottom end of the pattern firmly with your other hand.

Step 18: Twist Until A Rose-Like Pattern is Formed

Keep twisting until the origami rose is in full bloom. Once twisted firmly, the twist usually stays like that. But after making the twist, it is safe to arrange the layers with teh tip of your fingers. Just make sure not to pull any part too hard.

Step 18: Twist Until A Rose-Like Pattern is Formed

The first rose may not turn out to as nice, but that is totally fine. Grab a few more colored craft papers and practice making origami rose in bloom craft.

Origami Lily

What You'll Need

Materials

1 sheet square paper

Instructions

Make the First Folds

Start with your paper white side up if you have two-toned paper.

Fold the paper in half diagonally and unfold.

Fold the paper in half diagonally the other way and unfold.

You should now have two diagonal creases.

Flip and Fold

Flip the paper over.

Fold the paper in half as shown and unfold.

36

Fold the paper in half as shown.

Hold onto the bottom triangle and open out the top right area and bring it down to meet the bottom point.

Create a Square Base

Flatten out the crease in the center.

Squash the top section down. This is called a square base.

The open end needs to be at the top.

Fold one layer of the right edge into the middle as shown.

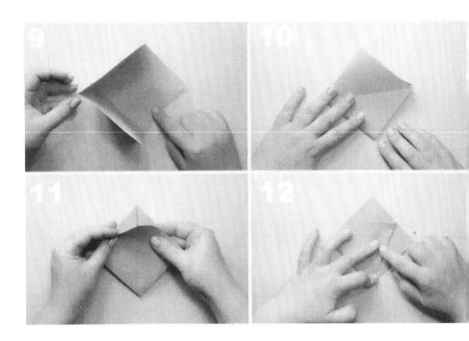

Fold to the Middle

Fold one layer of the left section to the middle as shown.

Open out the folds you just made.

Open out one layer from the right and flatten it out.

This should be what you have.

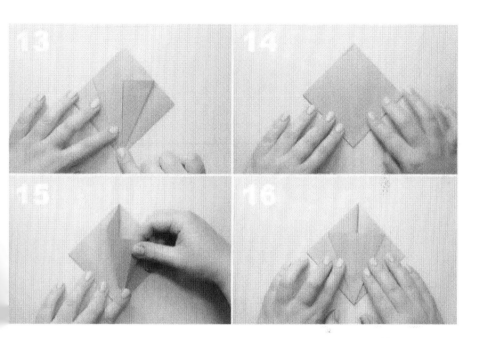

Repeat Three More Times

Do all the mini-steps in Step #4 for the remaining three layers.

Make sure the model looks like this—with the layers flipped so that you have the solid section.

Fold the right edge into the middle.

Fold the left edge into the middle.

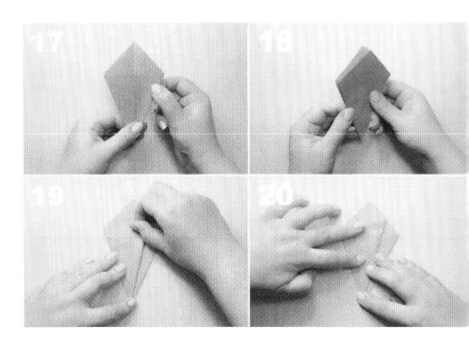

Complete the Flower

Fold the other three layers the same way.

Fold one layer from the top-down as far as it will go.

Fold the other three layers the same way.

Congratulations on a successful origami lily!

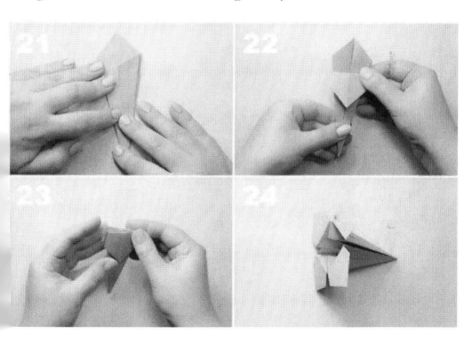

Easy Origami Flowers

Materials Needed:

Cardstock 12 x 12

Paper cutter

Bone folder

Paper straws

Buttons

Hot Melt Glue Gun

Cut paper into 3" squares. (you can use any size square, but this is the basic sized flower) If you use a 12" x 12", you can maximize your paper use.

Fold your paper square diagonally, bringing the bottom point to the top. Crease fold crisply; a bone folder works well and saves your fingers if you are making a lot.

Fold left and right points to top middle.

Fold those 2 triangles back onto themselves to the left and right.

5. I call this the tulip position. Open each side of the tulip and insert your finger.

6. Press down each side. Now they look like kites.

7. You can take your pick on this step. Fold the tops of the kites to the inside like in this pic. Your finished flower will then be showing the matching paper color on the inside, or

3. Fold the kite tops to the outside, which is probably easier if you are just getting started. The middles of your flowers will then be white, or whatever the back side of your paper is. If you look at all the finished

pictures of flowers in this post, you'll see the difference; see what you like better.

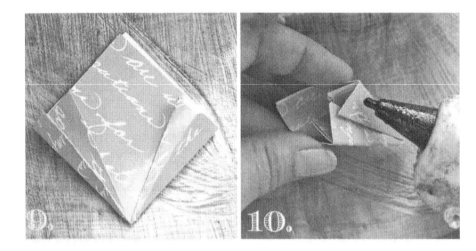

9. Now your folding is done. Make sure your hot glue gun is ready.

10. To make your petal, hot glue 2 inside triangles together and squeeze closed till dry. Do not squeeze or fold the cup part of the petal.

11. This is what your complete petal should look like.

12. To make a basic flower, you'll need 4, 5, or 6 petals.

Carnation Flower

Step 1: Fold a Square Paper Into an Equilateral Triangle Then the Kite Shape

You need 2-3 origami papers in any size. Stack them altogether and fold them into an equilateral triangle, then

Step 2: Make an Octagon

Step 3: Make the Saw for Your Carnation Petals

Step 4: Re-fold It and Shape an 8-petal Flower

Step 5: Make Your Carnation Flower Bloom!

Origami Hydrangea With Green Leaf Base

You will need:

16 pieces of square paper for the flowers (dimensions 3, 75 x 3, 75 cm). Or you can cut a 10 cm origami paper into four squares.

- One paper of square paper in green color, dimensions 15 x 15 cm.

- Glue

1. We'll begin with the flowers. Fold the paper diagonally both directions. Turn the paper over and fold in half both directions.

2. Bring the horizontal diagonal flaps to the centre so the model forms like a square and flatten.

3. Fold down the upper corner a bit. Then unfold.

4. Mountain fold on the creases that were made in the previous step.

 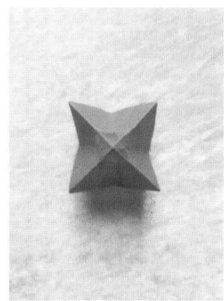

5. Fold it in by pushing the sides inwards.

5. Fold the right edge towards the middle line. Then move the left flap to the right and fold the right edge. Repeat this process on the backside.

7. Pull out all four petals and flatten. Then turn the model over.

8. Fold it down like in the pictures below.

). Fold the corners to shape the petals.

The flower is now completed. Make 15 more of these.

1. To make the base with leaves, fold the paper diagonally both directions and unfold.

2. Fold all four corners towards the middle and unfold.

 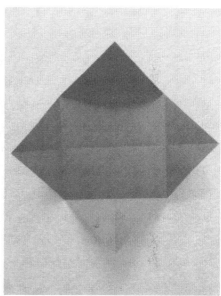

3. Fold all four the corners to the creases that were made in the previous step and unfold.

4. It should look like in the picture below.

5. Fold the two corners to the existing creases.

6. Turn the paper over and fold the upper two corners as you did in

the previous step.

7. Pinch it where the red marks are and then fold it in a bit on both sides. It should look like in the last picture in step 7.

9. Repeat for all corners.

10. Turn the paper over. Open up the two folded flaps and valley fold the paper where the red mark is.

11. Fold the right corner up to the red mark.

12. Fold the paper as a accordion to make the leaves.

13. Open up the paper and repeat step 10-12 to make the other leaf.

14. Open up the paper and fold in the two flaps in the existing creases

15. Fold the corners on the creases that were made in step 7. Repeat for all corners.

16. Fold in all the corners inside the base to lock it.

17. Gently pull out the leaves and then press where the red mark are.

18. Now it's time to glue the flowers. Start by gluing them around the bottom and move towards the middle.

19. The finished result.

Made in the USA
Columbia, SC
02 January 2025

51056019R00039